# SOMETIMES THE BIRDS COME BACK

ALSO BY NISHI PATEL

*The Inheritance of Grief*

# SOMETIMES THE BIRDS COME BACK

*Poetry & Prose by*

## Nishi Patel

First paperback edition 2025

ISBN 979-8-9862294-2-3 (paperback)
ISBN 979-8-9862294-3-0 (ebook)

Printed in the United States of America

Published by Nishi Patel
www.bynishipatel.com

*for my family*

# CONTENTS

All good things are wild and free.

—Henry David Thoreau

## SOME BEGINNING QUESTIONS

what happens after our last breath?
does healing start with death? would
the trees know? can
a flower simply be a flower? have
we been rotting under the surface all along?

## TODAY'S HIGH

the morning sun spills
partly through the clouds
and light accumulates inside
my body.  some people call this
healing.  I call it savoring some
goodness in a world full of
suffering.

# DISPLACEMENT

as a function of grief / it has been eight years since you
passed / feels like yesterday / means each year I say, feels
like only one year ago / means the gravity of grief is
accumulating / in a bar / means me / a jazz song / note by
note / until joy displaces the blues out of tune

to start again
to love again
is to live
again

and
again

# THIS IS NOT THE END

how many times I have felt
like I could not breathe
how my body has dropped
into the pit of grief like a stone
sinking, swallowed

how I am somehow still
able to emerge
from the great blue

and not end at drowning

## MIMOSA PUDICA
-the touch-me-not plant


I desire the light but
bend away from every possible
touch, then say *wait*
        *wait*
          *don't*
            *leave*
               *me*

## KITE

hope flew back
down a threaded thought

tethered to my soul
hello, grief

we both stood on a bridge
who will unspool next

# EMOTIONS AS BELONGINGS

there is nothing here
but a heart growing blue

so little it has left
so much it wants to contain

what else could I hold onto
if not you

# SWEET RUINS

am I the only one here
with dead things to hide

like fruit, left on the counter
ripening over and in itself

like feelings, kept in the body
eating away the flesh

am I the only one here
with dead things hiding

# A FIELD OF LOSS

what I know of loss
is that it fills up a whole body
like wildflowers in a field

leaves curl around my veins
roots press against
the walls of my skin

and petals b l o o m
into my lungs
where I gasp
         for air

## LET LOOSE

I want to inhabit space
outside my body
I want to dance
in a way that makes
paint splatter
across the
canvas of the room

don't you wonder
how one can exist
with so much grief
without shattering

# BODY

in the flesh / his, he left after 68 years old / father of mine /
is perhaps now a son a tree a bird / my brother, a body living
in Seattle, used to drive my father's 2013 Sonata / a body of
Hyundai / a body to a single disc cd player / a body to my
dad's favorite Hindi songs / timeless old tunes / always on /
always playing at very low volume / like background music
/ like the vibrational hum of a human being / alive like songs
of a heartbeat / and just like that I am about to lose him / all
over again / to take the cd out / to watch somebody come and
take this car from our home / it is no match for Kelley's blue
book / no match for a driver that is not my father or his son /
and then my mother says do not worry, I will play the cd in
my car now / as in a way to keep the beating on repeat / and
I could not help but think also in a way / reincarnation

*we are nothing but a symphony*
*of acting and reacting*

## GANESHA

could I please shed bad karma
could I please keep living
with a different face—
blessed and brave

# WHAT IS DONE, IS DONE

it pains me to wonder about all
the should have dones and all
the shouldn't have dones—
it is paralyzing and now
I am thinking the real
culprit is in the
wondering
itself—

halting any movement at all

as if the horizon is too heavy to meet the sun

## A LONELY JOURNEY

a day turns into another day
the sun no longer touches the horizon
happiness is a fleeting dream

I am calm but wash ashore angry
isolation has a way of accumulating
the hailstorm inside

have I told you I wish to touch the sun
its rays slip right through my fingers

those blackbirds, I envy how they sway
and disappear into the sky

# HUMAN

I build and I destroy
but I am never broken
I am living
learning
doing my best
even at my worst

# WINTER

there is something beautiful
in every womb of the night

a pain that stays
until you see the way

# ABSTRACT

the beauty of a just-finished
painting is not its completion
but how it is yet to be titled
that it is a whole and raw
body of work
and in this moment
it could be anything
and everything
all at once

## SELF-DEVELOPED

painting is
like processing film—
raw files extracted from
the darkroom of cellular memory
swell and unfurl onto
the flesh of canvas

# SELF-AWARENESS

meditate,
paint, bake,
practice ballet
or slow brew your next latte
whatever you love to do
try doing it without
any other distractions
inhabit a sacred space
to face the relationship
between you and yourself

# WE DON'T ALWAYS HAVE TO TALK ABOUT IT

you loving me
the way you do
gives my grief
a soft landing
spot to just be

not interrogating
and not abandoning me

grief never really goes away

neither does

*love*

neither does

*love*

# POROUS

there was a time when
I went to a studio
regularly for hot yoga
I invited my mother to join
and looked forward to the dripping
sweat soiling my clothes
it seemed sweating profusely
was the only way to purge
the grief that heavied me

now, as I stand on my mat
I ready myself for a gentle
morning routine right here
in the comfort of my home
my hands reach up and then down
to the ground I somehow make it
to downward dog and eventually
to plank
this is where
I hold
steady
as if gathering up
the weight of my grief on my back
I then bend my elbows slowly
lowering the plank of my body
to the ground

when the floor touches
my chest I cannot help but
remain there, forgetting

the next pose
it feels as if hands
from the ground are
reeling reeling reeling
the darkness out from my chest

# MOTHER EARTH

the only one strong enough
to caress a cemented heart
the only one gentle enough
to extract this gravity of grief

# A HABIT OF HARDNESS

when we treat our emotions
as belongings,
safely packed away
so not to lose those too,
we become
all bark and no leaves,
all land and no sea

# LESSON NOT LEARNED

why do I continue to get pricked
by the rose bush

prick
prick
blood

what lesson am I not learning

in this garden of life
full of thorns
I crave
your soft touch

## FORGIVENESS

forgiveness will treat you better
than revenge or resentment

it is freeing

for both the giver
and the receiver

who can both be you

-self love

# FORECAST

we met halfway
        between
a need and         a disappointment
        and still
     enough hope
        persists

# LANTANAS AND PURPLE SAGES

my brother-in-law tills the hardened
soil hoping to unbarren the earth that once grew
okras and baby eggplants. we are gifting
my dad a botanical garden. my only
request for every family member:
pick a perennial plant, preferably
one with bright blooms. that was the day
my father celebrated
his last birthday.    that was
9 years ago but the garden        the garden
overflows
       summer
          after
             every
                summer

# THE THINGS WE WANT

sometimes instead of wanting more
    we must want
        to be
           soft

I think too much
simmering until something makes sense
I seek   I seek   I seek
but my feelings are stronger than my thoughts
so I never find an answer
and end up going with instincts

# DISCONNECT TO CONNECT

I often think I know
how the answers go
they must be somewhere
in my mind
I am certain of this
as I am certain intelligence
is the only way
a brown girl
can make her way in life
but when I disconnect from my mind
and connect to nature
I remember the way blood
pulsates through a body
through *any* body
it just knows
and every time I am out
for a walk
a flower is there
staring back at me,
magnificently being
what it only knows—

how to be
open and brave
exuding a promise for life

## IN BLOOM

I looked out the window into my backyard
I thought they weren't going to survive
this scorching Texas heat
these myrtle trees
the dynamite ones
the ones with the crinkly flowers
intensely bursting with red
how stunningly they
hold to the branches
and from the branches they open
how they speak to the blood in my chest
that grief can bloom

without breaking

# ON A WALK

have you ever been on a walk,
gazing down towards your feet
with attention all up in your head?
you just need to spend
time with the trees,
a moment on the trail
to perspire your doubts

then all of a sudden,
a biker passes by
—on your left,
she says,
startling the stale
air in your lungs,
lifting your face
into a clearing,
a path
wide and green,
and now    now you feel
like you are actually
spending time with the trees

-being in-flow

# AT VILLAGE CREEK

tall trees line the concrete trail
where I walk, holding on to nothing

but questions. in my high school yearbook
a friend wrote in the 10-years-from-now page

that I would still be confused.
do the gods hear me? I think all the trees

are asking the same question wildly,
their bare limbs soaring high into the spring

light, the same way my arms reach up with wanting,
waiting for something good, like a blade

of bright grass.

I see yesterday's styrofoam cup
soaking in the riverbed, a swamp

collecting past regrets. there are
no pleasant distractions

from nature I come to seek, no singing
birds to raise a cheer in my spirits,

no blooming flowers to fruit
sweetness into my thoughts.

only stale browns and oh—the trees,
standing still in this windless hour.

in total exposure where the damage
falls, where the branches gracefully

bend, while the bough grows
proudly in its stark-naked stance

revealing a truth, I find my deepest
fear—how am I the only one here

     with something     to hide?

*trees do not have legs*
*but still a way to keep moving*

# WARNING

how do you know when the wilting
is an ending
to make room for new growth

how do you know when the wilting
is the beginning
of a terminal ending

## NATURE OF LIFE

there are no answers
except the ones from the trees
all around—they seem to be saying
I see where I am limited
I choose to keep growing
I will keep living
and even after standing straight, bending and gnarling
I find that an end is nearing
I then choose
to accept

# FIELD NOTES

leaning against the back door
coffee cupped against my chest
I find myself breathing    deeply—
watching her is like a field guide
frolicking into the flowers (or weeds)

I find the shape of her body
stretching onto the green lawn
curiosity like wings in the wind
bending the fabric of time

and I find myself thinking    thankful—
for people like her
to remind me

of how easy it is

to embrace

the simple nature            of joy

## WEEDS

my daughter only sees them as delights
tall flowering greens
speckled with yellows, purples and whites
what amazes me is not how they overtake
but how they do not have to try so hard

# SOUTHERN MAGNOLIA FLOWER

both male and female as One
white hearts uncurl their palms
to an offering—I cannot help but
stop and gaze at the flower's omnipresence
in jealousy of pollinating insects
needlelike pollens looking like
grains of rice each topped with a red tika
I bow my head
embody me—
embody me—
I too am a hungry wingless creature

# ON THIS WARM, MUGGY AUGUST AFTERNOON
in downtown Fort Worth

would you like it hot or cold?/ hot / I say without blinking
twice / the barista perks up / he tells me it has been a hybrid
day / an equal mix of customers ordering cold and hot
drinks / I am reminded of the other day when I ordered a
half salad and a half cold-cut sandwich / my summer-long
pick / you know, the usual / but the table next to mine
ordered a warm gooey baked potato / the voice of my belly
rumbles / it is interesting how the body knows the shifting
of seasons before the mind

## IN THE MIDDLE

when we are belly deep in slow days
change cannot come fast enough
and when disasters hit one after the other
we go through a rapid rate of transitions
before we even realize it

things don't feel like a change when we're in them
but are we not always standing in the middle of endings
and beginnings?

# OPENING THE PATH, AGAIN

summer's end is nearing
the routine starts again
I am dropping off my kid
to the first day of band camp
driving through the remnants
of last night's storm
a drastic change
from the Texas heat
startling and
screaming at us
roofs on fire
trees struck down
old and young
and this morning
it feels as if the sky is saying
are you awake yet
can your lungs feel
the crowdedness of
the fallen

August, not yet the end of summer
and not yet the beginning of fall

August, a long breath holding, stalling
at the threshold of release

August,
the bearer of grief

# LET THE SEASONS BE

this time I will not
stay in summer's
heat or wish for last spring
this time I will allow
myself to fall
gently on grief's shoulders
exhale the winter's
frost and ready my lungs
to grow forth

*nothing can change the earthly trials of life*

*we will never know the what-ifs*

*are we all just fruit*
*rotting on the table?*

# RESENTMENT

resentment is like a tree
it remembers deeply
grows profusely
(and won't quit)
the nature of it lives freely
like an evergreen
unless you intervene

-shed it

## SEPTEMBER'S SUN

it is a weird kind of warmth
when the pit of grief
settles into the bud
of September's sun
when the pain you feel
brushes against your skin
like autumn's brisk cool air
    like new breath
like hope on the other side
of gray skies

# OCTOBER

I fear that fall will quickly leave
as soon as it came
I want to stay here a while longer
before winter takes a stand on the other side of summer

because fall is      mild
not too hot, not too cold
it means eventually instead of extremes
which I know all too well
mostly the overwhelm and the depletion
too much or too little
all or nothing
I could use some mildness
in my bones
a gentle shedding of scars
not too rough
   and
      not too
            soft

## FALL BACK

do not rush forward / fall back / into a slower rhythm /
warm mugs and well-worn sweater season / harvest
summer-swept thoughts / tenderize like the skin of a red
pear / rest is found here / where acorns swell / where leaves
grow heavy and briefly bright / unhurried at the equinox of
change

## OVERFLOWING

when we are young
the future feels     forever
I will soon be     forty-four years old
and have been brewing on words lately,
simmering until something makes sense
compiling them into poems
which also means
trying to make wiser sense of my world

in all the twenty different versions of the same poem
I seek I seek I seek
until I am overflowing with thoughts
but none of it make any sense
so then I empty empty empty
clear my head     and repeat

this brain is intelligent but funny like that
some things just don't ever make enough sense
yet I pour another cup of coffee, drink, and think

tonight, the night is young and I am in bed
journaling while one daughter plays the piano
and the other draws in her sketchbook
after some time, I notice I can't hear them anymore
all the lights are still on
I find them in bed
falling asleep in each
other's arms, hair
still wet from their showers
fingers intertwined
bliss on their skin

from a day well spent

isn't that what matters?

to be   more in our hearts
than our heads?

to fill   an entire day with moments
that feel like
                forever?

# A DEATH IN THE FAMILY

who am I
to keep dried flowers and winter
berries in beautiful glass vases—
shapes of the dead displayed
in an open casket
I tossed them all out
gave back what belongs to the birds,
to the earth—to the
life givers

## APRICITY
/a-PRIS-i-tee/

today I learned a new ancient word: apricity
it means the warmth of the sun in winter
like one season seeping into the other
hope warming a wearied heart
a very familiar concept
but we don't often use the word apricity in our language
we are familiar with grief but don't speak of it enough
let's talk about grief more so we can also
talk about the apricity of it

# UNFROZEN

I have finally learned
to hold my heart like petals,
opening towards the sun,
tears slipping over the edge

## ALL SEASONS

I have seen flowers bloom in the fall and winter
I have seen flowers die in the spring and summer
there is growth and there is grief
in all seasons of life

# RESILIENCE

let me feel no limits
when grief revisits

let me be burning deep in despair
let me be wildflowers everywhere

## CURRENT

are we not constantly fluctuating
between two versions of ourselves
the one who feels everything
and the other who exists less
in our own body
coping just enough to be able to return
to our original selves with more
capacity to hold

I am still learning to
ask for what I need
but one thing I now know for sure
is asking for help
does not make me any less strong

## CAMOUFLAGED HUMAN

covered in moon dust
hanging on the cliffside of grief
I am something like a bastion
of a geode
a delayed opening
with a story inside to tell

# LIKE A MILLION HANDS WAVING

a weeping willow is swaying in the wind
    whispering through the branches
and casting its shadows on the earth
    while reaching for the sun

listen in and around the silence
    when someone shares their grief with you
the thousand words more
    left unsaid
invisible hands waving
    for your attention

their whispers and shadows
    are trying really hard to reach you

# THE VIEW

an article I read about cicadas
said their exoskeletons are tangible
shadows of their former selves
imagine if we too
could split our backs
   in the face of night
for our soft bodies
   to crawl out
turn around and witness grief
         in the past tense

I am not thinking
about what my future self
would say to my present self
I am gazing up at the stars
in awe of the person I was
that got me here today

-reflect on the amazing person you already are

today's moon phase is
losing the last of its glow
I tell myself, go to sleep now, be
new tomorrow

-self-doubt

I remind myself
that trying to heal
all the time
is like facing a full moon
every single day—
it floods the heart

a sliver might be just enough
to cut through the dark

-slow progress

like the moon
I am always changing—
slightly different
day by day

# A CHANCE WORTH TAKING

hope is a dandelion seed
a wish blown in the wind
coming back
to land on your skin

*if there is a chance*
*there is hope*

*but hope did not get me here*
*I got here because it also meant believing*

*I got here because believing*
*also moved me to take small steps*
*towards my goal*

# INVITATION

I am painting again
slowly inviting back in
the things I used to love

I drew myself a bath
made a second cup of tea
and did not feel guilty
for taking space just for me

an empty body
longs to be full and
a banished person endlessly roams—
both searching for a welcome home

# NEW HOPE

my eyes wake up to
clouds yawning in the sky
sun hazing through the other side

## SOLITUDE

I like to be alone with the earth's greens and blues
it helps me view my grief at a distance
it gives me a ground to fall on and a sky to cast away in

# WHERE THE WIND TAKES YOU

you see, we keep returning
to the elements of nature
tethering
to the sun when we want light
and untethering
into the sea when we want
to feel free
the trick is knowing how not
to burn and drown
in our desires and misery

# HOW TO TRAVEL

the first origami
I ever made
was a boat
taught by my
dad
who loved to show me
how to in our old home

the last origami
I made was
a crane
I taught him
how to in
the waiting room

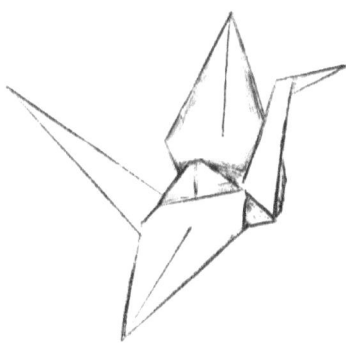

# FULFILLED

when I am old
let happiness be
as content as a gentle stream
as warm as earth after
the sun goes down
and thought, rising like a moon

# PRANAYAMA

life in lines and
then the stanza breaks

and holds, waiting
waiting waiting

I found a place between
day and night where

stories from an art museum
rests on benches

so much freedom
is gained in the regulation

of rhythm, of breath
breath breath

*I feel like I know more than I think I know
how space contains more stars than we can see*

# HUMIDITY

I think a lot about
prayers and sunrises
how not to come undone
when we expand
how to become wider and
wider like lungs full
of breath, a body full
of air carrying less weight
to become water vapor
to become
cold air rising

## COLD AIR RISING

joy is rising / means I am learning
how to car^ry
        myself
  above deserted grounds

despite all the grief I inherit
I am learning how to feel

r
   e
  t
h
g
i
l

# THE GOOD DARK

have patience,
look on,
the stars will come out
to shine for you

## STARLIGHT

I am here in this darkness
of grief awaiting the dawn
of its starlight wings

one day when you reach a bottom
that is the darkest of blacks
know that it is also
the merging of
all colors

## SUNSETS AND FIREWORKS

alone on the beach
a dying day closes in on me

an out-of-tune loneliness
crescendos against the silence of my skin
a wave rises over itself
until nothingness erupts
            collapsing
               onto the elongated shore

but then
a splash of surprise
rockets over the sea
a fountain of lights
fills the dark sky
and the pounding
        floods through my veins
dreams
        tail like comets and
                    linger
long after the fireworks end

it is pitch dark but darkness
no longer consumes the sky
I remember the sun
        it rises on my face

*grief is an eclipse of happiness*

like the sky, we are never completely dark
we are never completely void of starlight

## STARDUST

have you ever felt like the sun
is smiling back at you
or is it from your eyes—
a beaming light you feel inside,
like stardust, a power
from the happiness burning in disguise

*release* your energies like stars

## HAPPINESS

I once found it
bunched in giggles

released from my children
like songbirds in the air

catch them catch them
one by one
a collection of happiness

my chest, a keepsake box

when the lights die
what is left but a hoarding
of memory and thought

a yearning

an idea is just an idea
a pearl in a protected shell

luster waiting to be unveiled

♥

in fact, there is no place
in the body for this bright
beautiful thing that is
         meant to linger
                  in the air
to live without possession

♥

lightweight
golden
far away from the
gravity of need

♥

a wind of satisfaction
a clearing for more

♥

sometimes the birds come back

# SOMETIMES THE BIRDS COME BACK

allowing the wings of happiness to fly
keeps its heartbeat alive

# BIRDS

they remember locations of sustenance
stored food and home
your primate incarnation
gone only days ago

a bird swiftly perches outside
my second-story window
on the other side of the glass
sits my pulsating heart

## MEMORIES AND EVERY PRECIOUS THING

what will remain after the birds fade
into the bright light

who will carry memory
like a pearled necklace
        to hand it
            down
            down
            down
                in lineage

# TOOTH FAIRIES

I watch and wrestle with a secret
a myth and yet still
marvel at her marveling

like today as she unscrolls the letter
and catches the gold coin
I should tell her the truth

about tooth fairies but instead
I push the button to the moon roof.
through the rear-view mirror

I glimpse her big
brown eyes, brilliant
as the spilling proof of light

filtering in like glitter
how they also make my—
I wonder

who else is this secret for
perhaps it's less than fair to—
I guess

the real struggle is
having to always be in the driver's seat
perhaps the real magic is

having a ceiling that uncovers
almost the entire roof
perhaps—it is better

to leave the window open
to pockets full of wonder
a little longer
in this harsh harsh world

# BONFIRE OF DESIRE

I want to feel
the expanse above low horizons
where sacred forest trees are the only skyscrapers
and boredom is felt in my bare bones

I want it quiet enough
to hear the universe tug
on the blood of my heart
and watch my cells pulse     without fear

# VINYASA

yoga is my form of devotion
where the energy of the universe
guides my moving meditation

# YES, THERE IS SUNLIGHT AND OXYGEN OUT HERE

but first, I turn to myself
reaching for my core
the way trees know how to ground
down, drawing
nourishment from the earth

this source of power
is fuel
it needs to be found
before it can turn into fire

# AGNI

every now and then,
come away from the high
center down
      from the beautiful wild
   reign in
from running into that delightful dawn
          the rush
     the wind
  and the swallowing sea

you see, discipline isn't always
about controlling the wanting
nor is it self-limiting to the soul
it is about
      cultivating
   fire
and knowing where
        to let it burn

## SPRING FORWARD

do not fall back / into old habits of last season / look at the bright daffodils / the first call of spring / look at the dollops of violet hyacinths / the cups of tulips brimming to the rim / the rays of sunshine / fresh rain / the pouring of the past / the sprouts of the new / lily pads emerging / frogs jumping / the daffodils now droop / but look, look at the other green buds anew

# AURA

morning meets a smile,
my whole face aglow
from the dream.  love
wraps around my body
my body is wrapped in a blanket
everything expands from the inside out
this must be self-love, I think
allowing gentleness to grow
and reenter

## BOUNDLESS

I think also about the people
who carried love for me
from before

from you
old friends
my dead father
I was in his house
he was alive and well

he was in his yellow
collared shirt and khaki pants
he says there is a problem with the thermostat, and
although he rambled on and on, I

stood back and nodded in a simple sweet gaze
I was aware
(of the fluctuation of time)

I soaked in his hair
he in the past and I in the future

and this, this is okay

I see now

a love which seems
boundless at the time, disappears

but today, today it feels timeless

sometimes you have to stand
back from your artwork
to see it as a whole
body of work—
see how it catches the light

stand back and
see yourself from a distance
how you too shine bright

## ARTIST'S STATEMENT

when an idea finds my mind
I cannot help
the way it takes over my body—
the way light
expands over the world

## ALIVE

let me feel most alive
like the sun
and the rain—
vibrant and freefalling

# 9 WAYS TO STAY ALIVE
after Daphne Gottlieb

Grieve because even the sun casts a shadow.
Clear up space. Donate things you don't need. You don't
have room for bullshit either.
Dance, kiss, laugh—in the rain.
Hug tightly and a little longer, long after the resistance of
leaning into the hug fades.
Sit outside and use your eyes to observe and your nose to
breathe; don't say anything.
Run something soft through your fingers: a blanket, a
t-shirt, the hair of someone you love.
Sing—loudly.
Feel happiness from the happiness you know you made
someone else feel.
Forgive because resentment will eat you alive.

# THE HEART THAT REMAINS

you can find my heart
in places and people
in poems and paintings
you can find my heart
in belongings displayed
all over my home
you could take away all these things
but never the story
which always stays alive
even if not you
even if not me

## THE AFTERLIFE

detached from bonds underneath the skin
you are now free to roam the universe

# POEMS

poems do not have final
destinations or endings
they are like aged leaves
                    memories
lingering in the wind

they are the earth
that holds
even after bodies decompose

they are sprouts
pulling from the past
  in a new light

poems are cycles of life
that rebirth again
                and again
                    and again

# PLANETARY ALIGNMENT HAPPENS MORE FREQUENTLY THAN WE THINK

life is short
and we are too busy to see
the many sightings
out there and even
the precious moments
down here
life is short and we are too busy
to see how often we humans
are in alignment with each other

# HANUMAN

when doubt floods my capacity to carry on
and all I want to do is crumble onto the floor
I remember the people whose words are
balm to my wounded self-esteem—
friends who lift the fog so I can see
how I have always been able to move
mountains and persevere

and as I think of you
I know somewhere someone
thinks of me
as an avatar of strength

# WISDOM

I have listened to the breath
between the leaves of the trees
I now have answers
and even more questions

# UNTITLED

what is a titleless poem
an illness a garden a person
without a word to be known
such a simple act
to honor a thing
a House Sparrow
the Pacific Ocean
my name and
suddenly the world makes
a little more sense

# THE PRESENT MOMENT

gaze straight ahead
at this very moment
see the landscape of the present
in all shades of life—
the grays and the brights

# SYNCHRONY

and when you sit to play
the piano
all words melt away
we are once again
united in a ballad
of songbirds

## EPIC

a lifetime is one long epic poem
make it count

I am certain
that it is up to me now
to be gentle—
to exude a promise
                    for life

# GLOSSARY

*Ganesha*, p. 17. [guh · nay · shah]
the elephant-headed Hindu deity / remover of obstacles /
god of wisdom and success

*tika*, p. 48. [tee · kaa]
a mark generally made on the forehead / "Southern
Magnolia Flower" references the red powder and rice used
on the forehead of a devotee, seeking blessings

*pranayama*, p. 85. [prah · na · ya · ma]
*prana*: "life-force" *yama*: "control"
the exercise of breath regulation / this poem refers to the
"box breathing" technique

*vinyasa*, p. 108. [vin · yaa · sa]
vi: "in a special way" nyasa: "to place"
a yoga practice with fluid transitions from one pose to
another along with the alignment of the breath, body, and
mind

*agni*, p. 110 [ahg · nee]
the sanskrit word for fire

*Hanuman*, p.122. [huh · noo · maan]
the Hindu deity of strength, courage, and devotion

# NOTES & ACKNOWLEDGMENTS

"Some Beginning Questions" was inspired by Victoria Chang's poem, "Some Last Questions" from *The Trees Witness Everything*.

"Body" was selected to appear in the *Central Avenue Poetry Prize 2025*.

"In Bloom" was first published in The Poetry Club Magazine by Shelby Leigh.

"Humidity" and "Cold Air Rising" was written after reading the Life Science article, *Sometimes, cool air rises. Here's what that means for tropical climates*.

"9 Ways to Stay Alive" was written in response to a prompt after Daphne Gottlieb's poem, "15 Ways to Stay Alive".


Thank you to Shelby Leigh, whose keen eye exceeds my expectations. I am truly grateful for the multiple rounds of editing that helped shape this collection into its finest form. Thank you to William Bortz and Taylor Byas for allowing me to borrow your eyes on select poems. Your unique perspective and detailed feedback are much appreciated. Thank you to all my peers and fellow poets who read early versions of these poems, providing invaluable insights, and undoubtedly cheering me on every step of the way.

Thank you to Islam Farid for your artistic ability to capture the essence of this poetry collection into a beautiful book cover. Thank you to Beau Adler and Michelle Halket at Central Avenue Publishing for selecting and publishing one of my poems in the 2025 Poetry Prize Collection. This is truly an honor.

A heartfelt thank you to my friends, my family, my daughters, and my husband for all the memories and experiences we share together. No matter how big or small the moment, it is deeply cherished.

Many thanks to you, my dear readers, for embarking on this poetic journey with me.

I bow humbly to you, Mother Earth, for your wisdom.

# ABOUT THE BOOK

How does one navigate a life forward after being lost and
stagnant with grief? With a longing for answers, Nishi
Patel's second poetry collection is wonderous and
philosophical. *Sometimes the Birds Come Back* is an
inquisitive journey interrogating the nature of death and the
meanings of life with the possibility of finding happiness
again.

Complete with hand-drawn illustrations, *Sometimes the
Birds Come Back* is a meditation on the beauty and grace of
the natural world, noticing the cyclical nature of grief, and
rekindling our relationships with oneself, the people we
love, and the earth we live on. In these poems, memories,
grief, happiness, and longing are all fields of gold.

Nishi Patel is a visual artist and author. Her work explores many facets of emotions such as the duality of grief and joy. She is the author of *The Inheritance of Grief*, her debut poetry book. Nishi's acrylic paintings are exhibited throughout her local public communities. She lives in Fort Worth, Texas where she loves spending quality time with her family, drinking a cup of hot mocha, and finding solace in the beauty of nature.